TO: Joann

From Donna

Christmas 2002

Glad You're My Friend

Kim Jacobs

HARVEST HOUSE™ PUBLISHERS

EUGENE, OREGON

Introduction

Friendship is a walk on the beach, a pot of tea shared, a task completed together, and so much more!

It is a living thing—ever growing and changing. It manifests itself in its own way at different times and places. At times it flowers and at times it rests. At times it takes and at times it gives. And like all living things, it needs to be nurtured and yet it gives nurture too.

Friendship is also like an exquisite jewel, forged and clarified by the fires of life. If we observe it carefully, we see a myriad of facets in its ever-changing face; the world reflected in it, ourselves reflected in it. What a precious thing! May we cherish it always...

If instead of a gem, or even a flower, we should cast the gift of loving thought into the heart of a friend, that would be giving as the angels give.

George MacDonald

Friendship is...

A day at the beach

*I*t is special places of beauty and wonder shared—where each individual's unique way of observing the world enhances the other's.

"We will go—you and I alone, Caroline—early some fine summer morning, and spend a long day there. We can take pencils and sketch books, and any interesting readingbook we like..." "I shall like to go, Shirley," again said Miss Helstone. "I long to hear the sound of waves—ocean waves, and to see them as I have imagined them in dreams, like tossing banks of green light, strewed with vanishing and reappearing wreaths of foam, whiter than lilies."

Charlotte Brontë
Shirley

I have made friends with the sea; it has taught me a great deal. There is a kind of inspiration in the sea. When one listens to its never-ceasing murmur afar out there, always sounding at midnight and mid-day, one's soul goes out to meet Eternity.

L.M. Montgomery
Along the Shore

And we find at the end of a perfect day, the soul of a friend we've made. Carrie Jacobs Bond

Friendship is...

A mountain excursion

There are journeys and places unknown by one, yet of special interest to another, becoming the delight of both.

They clung to this scene, I say, with a perfect enthusiasm of attachment. I could comprehend the feeling, and share both its strength and truth. I saw the fascination of the locality...my eye feasted on the outline of swell and sweep on the wild colouring communicated to ridge and dell, by moss, by heath-bell, by flower-sprinkled turf, by brilliant bracken, and mellow granite crag. These details were just to me what they were to them—so many pure and sweet sources of pleasure. The strong blast and the soft breeze; the rough and the halcyon day; the hours of sunrise and sunset; the moonlight and the clouded night, developed for me, in these regions, the same attraction as for them—wound round my faculties the same spell that entranced theirs.

Charlotte Brontë
J A N E   E Y R E

If the sight of the blue skies fills you with joy, if a blade of grass springing up in the fields has power to move you, if the simple things of nature have a message that you understand, rejoice, for your soul is alive...

Eleonora Duse

n Jacobs ©

Friendship is...

A market day together

*W*hen work is shared...

~ weighty tasks are made light

~ decisions are made easy

~ time forfeited to mundane chores becomes time gained for companionship.

And work is made fun by virtue of being shared with one whose company is a joy.

Friendship is a strong and habitual inclination in two persons to promote the good and happiness in one another.
Eustace Budgell

Man's best support is a very dear friend.
Cicero

Two are better than one, because they have a good return for their work: If one falls down, his friend can help him up. But pity the man who falls and has no one to help him up!
The Book of Ecclesiastes

Friends are the sunshine of life. *John Hay*

Friendship is...

Preparing a meal to share

*I*t is satisfaction of time spent creating what one knows will please, the joy in anticipation...and the fulfillment of sitting down together and seeing the promise of that pleasure realized.

Get not your friends by bare compliments, but by giving them sensible tokens of your love.
Socrates

God loveth a cheerful giver.
The Book of 2 Corinthians

Lord, grant that our time together be steeped in serenity, sweetened by sharing, and surrounded by the warm fragrance of your love.
Emilie Barnes

Friendship is...

Taking tea together

With soothing tastes and a welcoming setting, things can be talked of that need talking of. Here one can be truly available to listen or, with trust in the other's attention, speak of one's own concerns and dreams.

The mind never unbends itself so agreeably as in the conversation of a well-chosen friend. There is indeed no blessing of life that is any way comparable to the enjoyment of a discreet and virtuous friend. It eases and unloads the mind, clears and improves the understanding, engenders thought and knowledge, animates virtue and good resolutions, soothes and allays the passions, and finds employment for most of the vacant hours of life.

Joseph Addison

"I can just imagine myself sitting down at the head of the table and pouring out the tea," said Anne, shutting her eyes ecstatically. "And asking Diana if she takes sugar! I know she doesn't but of course I'll ask her just as if I didn't know."

L.M. Montgomery
Anne of Green Gables

Somehow, taking tea together encourages an atmosphere of intimacy when you sleep off the timepiece in your mind and cast your fate to a delight of tasty tea, tiny foods, and thoughtful conversation.

Gail Greco

My Birdhouse

KimJacobs©

Friendship is...

A welcome visit

*I*t is making time in a busy life to show that: "Yes, time with you is important to me."

The pleasure of your company is a many-sided affair. It includes the pleasure of seeing you, the pleasure of hearing you talk, the drama of watching your actions, your likes and dislikes and adventures; the pleasure of hunting you up in your haunts, and the delicate flattery we feel when you hunt us up in ours.

Frances Lester Warner

Go oft to the house of thy friend, for weeds choke the unused path.

Ralph Waldo Emerson

A true friend is the gift of God, and he only who made hearts can unite them.

Robert South

Friendship increases in visiting friends.
Author Unknown

Friendship is...

Young hearts forging a lifelong bond

*I*t is the wondrous headlong new attachment of childhood, as well as the marvelous endurance of a lifelong bond.

The new friendship is...
- ~ quick, accepting, and uncomplicated
- ~ delicate, but growing more vigorous day by day.

The old is...
- ~ steady, deep, and complex
- ~ strong, but bending with what life brings.

The new...
- ~ flush with the excitement of the unexplored—a journey begun.

The old...
- ~ content in the comfort of the well-known—a safe haven reached.

In the first, the precious promise of the second.

Outside in the garden, which was full of mellow sunset light streaming through the dark old firs to the west of it, stood Anne and Diana, gazing bashfully at one another over a clump of gorgeous tiger lilies...

"Oh, Diana," said Anne at last, clasping her hands and speaking almost in a whisper, "do you think—oh, do you think you can like me a little—enough to be my bosom friend?"

Diana laughed. Diana always laughed before she spoke.

"Why, I guess so," she said frankly. "I'm awfully glad you've come to live at Green Gables. It will be jolly to have somebody to play with."

L.M. Montgomery
Anne of Green Gables

Yes'm old friends is always best 'less you can catch a new one that's fit to make an old one out of.

Sarah Orne Jewet

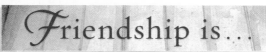

Friendship is...

Wonderful leisure time spent together

*H*ere we find a playful opponent in challenges of mind and skill, an inspiration to new areas of learning and enjoyment, and a sharing of talents and thoughts. In game, sport, arts, and scholarship...we have a companion in winning and losing, failure and success, and in expressing opinions without fear of ridicule or censure.

And in friendship we gain an ally in our challenge to focus on the essential, the vital, and the meaningful in the myriad of opportunities that life has to offer.

To have a good friend is one of the highest delights of life; to be a good friend is one of the noblest and most difficult undertakings.
                    Author Unknown

Of all the things which wisdom provides to make life entirely happy, much the greatest is the possession of friendship.
                    Epicurus

A man with few friends is only half-developed; there are whole sides of his nature which are locked up and have never been expressed. He cannot unlock them himself, he cannot even discover them; friends alone can stimulate him and open him.
                    Randolph Bourne

Perhaps the most delightful friendships are those in which there is much agreement, much disputation, and yet more personal liking.
                    George Eliot

Friendship is...

A dream of chocolate shared

An accomplice in delightful indulgences
A confederate in merry surprises
A champion of timely lightheartedness
And best of all...a partner in laughter

What a glorious gift to the heart are the simple pleasures shared!

———————————— ∞ ————————————

Congeniality, when once established between two kindred spirits or in a group, is the most carefree of human relationships. It is effortless, like purring. It is a basic theme in friendship...
Frances Lester Warner

Wear a smile and have friends; wear a scowl and have wrinkles.
George Eliot

We cherish our friends not for their ability to amuse us, but for ours to amuse them.
Evelyn Waugh

Wake up with a smile
and go after life...
Live it, enjoy it, taste
it, smell it, feel it.
Joe Knapp

Friends are the most important ingredient in the recipe of life. Author Unknown

Friendship is...

A teatime rendezvous for treats with a special companion

The simple yet essential act of nourishment is so intertwined with the idea of friendship that from this unique relationship one of the foremost names for friend is born—*companion*.

From the root words *com*, meaning "together," and *panis*, meaning "bread," the word *companion* literally means "one who breaks bread with another." What a beautiful definition!

So long as we love, we serve; so long as we are loved by others, I should say that we are almost indispensable; and no man is useless while he has a friend.

Robert Louis Stevenson

Strange to see how a good dinner and feasting reconciles everybody.

Samuel Pepys

The feeling of friendship is like that of being comfortably filled with roast beef...

Samuel Johnson

Rows of spotless plates winked from the shelves of the dresser at the far end of the room, and from the rafters overhead hung hams, bundles of dried herbs, nets of onions, and baskets of eggs. It seemed a place where heroes could fitly feast after victory, where weary harvesters could line up in scores along the table and keep their Harvest Home with mirth and song, or where two or three friends of simple tastes could sit about as they pleased and eat and talk in comfort and contentment.

Kenneth Grahame
The Wind in the Willows

Friendship is...

A home-baked pie for someone special

friend, with memories of happy times and thoughts shared to guide them, can create that simple gift of the heart that so suits and satisfies.

We secure our friends not by accepting favors but by doing them.
Thucydides

I made all the gifts...I hope you will like your watch-case, for it made me very happy to make it for you.
Helen Keller

Verily great grace may go with a little gift; and precious are all things that come from friends.
Theocritus

Give her the fruit of her hands; and let her own works praise her in the gates.
The Book of Proverbs

Thus nature has no love for solitude, and always leans, as it were, on some support; and the sweetest support is found in the most intimate friendship. Cicero

Friendship is...

Sharing in the delights of gardening

The garden itself is like friendship. It needs work to thrive and, in return, offers nourishment and great delight through its beauty. Careful observation attunes us to its needs. We see when it needs feeding and when it needs cultivating, and when conditions are difficult, we see even more care and attention are needed. With growth, some things flourish side by side, appreciating the support that closeness brings, while others need more room to expand in different directions.

At times the garden rests, full of potential. And then, when the season is right, it gathers impetus in its growing and bursts forth with all its bounty!

———————————— ∾ ————————————

He was working all the time he was talking and Mary was following him and helping him with her fork or the trowel.

"There's a lot of work to do here!" he said once, looking about quite exultantly. "Will you come again and help me do it?" Mary begged. "I'm sure I can help, too. I can dig and pull up weeds, and do whatever you tell me. Oh! Do come, Dickon!" "I'll come every day if tha' wants me, rain or shine," he answered stoutly. "It's th' best fun I ever had in my life—shut in here an' wakenin' up a garden."

Frances Hodgson Burnett
The Secret Garden

A friendship can weather most things and thrive in thin soil, but it needs just a little mulch of letters and phone calls and small, silly presents every so often—just to save it from drying out completely.

Pam Brown

Friendship is . . .

A peaceful courtyard shared

*I*t's a place of comfortable understanding established in the company of an attentive and sympathetic listener. That precious listener's capacity for a clear understanding is grounded in a willingness to step away from their own safe and familiar perspective, in a willingness to stand side by side with the other to view the world from the other's vantage. In this way it becomes possible to give the proper weight to what another values, though differing from our reality.

With clear understanding comes a true sharing of feelings. And so where feelings are troubling, there is a burden lightened, and where uplifting, there is joy multiplied!

If you want to be listened to, you should put in time listening.
Marge Piercy

A real friend is one who walks in when the rest of the world walks out.
Walter Winchell

The secret to friendship is being a good listener. *Author Unknown*

Friendship is...

A letter signed with affection

With thoughts reaching toward a distant dear one, a hand travels across a page, creating a packet of rich communication, a sharing of thought and feeling with a clarity difficult to achieve through spoken words. A letter transcends time and space to find its welcoming presence able to be savored again and again—a small miracle of transported affection.

The next morning a note, most fearfully and wonderfully twisted and folded, and a small parcel, were passed across to Anne.

"Dear Anne," ran the former, "Mother says I'm not to play with you or talk to you even in school. It isn't my fault and don't be cross at me, because I love you as much as ever. I miss you awfully to tell all my secrets to and I don't like Gertie Pye one bit. I made you one of the new bookmarkers out of red tissue paper. They are awfully fashionable now and only three girls in school know how to make them. When you look at it remember
"Your true friend, Diana Barry."

Anne read the note, kissed the bookmark, and dispatched a prompt reply back to the other side of the school.

"My own darling Diana:—

"Of course I am not cross at you because you have to obey your mother. Our spirits can commune. I shall keep your lovely present forever. Minnie Andrews is a very nice little girl although she has no imagination but after having been Diana's busum friend I cannot be Minnie's. Please excuse mistakes because my spelling isn't very good yet, although much improved.

"Yours until death us do part, Anne or Cordelia Shirley.

"P.S. I shall sleep with your letter under my pillow tonight. A. or C.S."

L.M. Montgomery
Anne of Green Gables

Friendship is...

A seaside retreat shared

When we find someone we can let ourselves be vulnerable with, we will find...

~ a companion in truthfulness, like a cleansing sea breeze
~ one to whom you can tell the truth
~ someone who will tell the truth to us when asked and, sometimes, when not asked but needed
~ one who will disagree respectfully, not taking the easy course when the truth is difficult to share

True friendship is not about appearances. It does away with pretenses, dispensing with artificiality and freeing us to show our real selves.

True friendship does not muddle...it brings clarity. How refreshing!

———

Your words came just when needed.
Like a breeze
Blowing and bringing from the
Wide soft sea
Some cooling spray, to meadow
Scorched with heat
And choked with dust and clouds
Of sifted sand...
So words of thine came over
Miles to me,
Fresh from the mighty sea, a
True friend's heart,
And brought me hope, strength,
And swept away
The dusty webs that human
Spiders spun
Across my path, Friend and
The word mean much—
So few there are who reach
like thee, a hand...

Ella Wheeler Cox

Friendship is...

A company of players

*I*t is a fellowship—a union of equals—where each one helps the other to excel in their part. Taken together, a wonderfully satisfying whole is created. How wonderful to find friends who encourage us to step forward and speak out, who rehearse us through our difficult passages, and who are found behind the scenes in silent support or out in front applauding us!

The primary joy of life is acceptance, approval, the sense of appreciation and companionship of our human comrades. Many men do not understand that the need for fellowship is really as deep as the need for food, and so they go throughout life accepting many substitutes for genuine, warm, simple relatedness.

Joshua Loth Liebman

A friend is someone who knows the song in your heart, and can sing it back to you when you have forgotten the words.

Author Unknown

Hearts are linked to hearts by God. The friend on whose fidelity you can count, whose success in life flushes your cheek with honest satisfaction, whose triumphant career you have traced and read with a heart throbbing almost as if it were a thing alive, for whose honor you would answer as for your own—that friend, given to you by circumstances over which you have no control, was God's own gift.

Frederic William Robertson

But there is a
friend that sticks
closer than a brother.
*The Book of
Proverbs*

From quiet homes
and first beginning,
Out to the
undiscovered ends,
There's nothing
worth the wear
of winning,
But laughter and
the love of friends.
Hilaire Belloc

Friendship is...

A good scratch

A playful gesture of affection

A touch of the hand
A kiss on the cheek
A hug

One who knows how to show and to accept kindness will be a friend better than any possession.
Sophocles

As the two boys walked sorrowing along, they made a new compact to stand by each other and be brothers and never separate till death relieved them of their troubles.
Mark Twain
The Adventures of Tom Sawyer

Piglet had got up early that morning to pick himself a bunch of violets; and when he had picked them and put them in a pot on the middle of his house, it suddenly came over him that nobody had ever picked Eeyore a bunch of violets, and the more he thought of this, the more he thought how sad it was to be an Animal who had never had a bunch of violets picked for him. So he hurried out again, saying to himself, "Eeyore, Violets," and then "Violets, Eeyore," in case he forgot, because it was that sort of day.
A.A. Milne
The House at Pooh Corner

Friendship is...

A playmate

What was quiet enjoyment for one becomes joyful play for two...
The miraculous power of paired imagination transforms the commonplace into settings for dreams and grand escapades.

Happy engagement brings blissful absorption in the moment...

And two together bring each other the wholesome gifts of diversion and laughter.

In reality, we are still children. We want to find a playmate for our thoughts and feelings.
Dr. Wilhelm Stekhel

It is great to have friends when one is young, but indeed it is still more so when you are getting old. When we are young, friends are, like everything else, a matter of course. In the old days we know what it means to have them.
Edvard Grieg

It takes a long time to grow an old friend.
Author Unknown

ℱriendship is...

A rainy day walk together

𝒜 good friend is someone we can feel comfortable with and seek comfort from, one to share the dark days with as well as the bright. We can share not only our dreams, but our nightmares, worries, fears, and failures...and by sharing and showing them, we dispel them like clouds before a warming sun.

***

It was the best thing she could have said. To talk about Dickon meant to talk about the moor and about the cottage and the fourteen people who lived in it on sixteen shillings a week—and the children who got fat on the moor grass like the wild ponies. And about Dickon's mother—and the skipping rope—and the moor with the sun on it—and about pale green points sticking up out of the black sod. And it was all so alive that Mary talked more than she had ever talked before—and Colin both talked and listened as he had never done either before. And they both began to laugh over nothing as children will when they are happy together. And they laughed so that in the end they were making as much noise as if they had been two ordinary, healthy, natural, two-year-old creatures...

Frances Hodgson Burnett
The Secret Garden

We cannot hold a torch to light another's path without brightening our own. *Ben Sweetland*

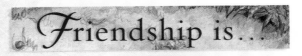

Friendship is...

A task shared

*I*t is help freely given...and help gladly received.

Friends are helpmates, providing each other aid not only in lightening the weight of work, but with alleviating the anxieties of mundane problems and even in confronting our innermost dilemmas.

In a helpmate is an offer of a clear eye seeing a new perspective, of a fresh mind finding new solutions, and of eager hands adding vital energy toward a happy resolution.

And perhaps best of all, it is the heartening knowledge that there is someone there for us, who is not only willing to be called upon, but who feels gratified in being asked.

If I can stop one heart from breaking,
I shall not live in vain;
If I can ease one life the aching,
Or cool one pain,
Or help one fainting robin
Unto his nest again,
I shall not live in vain.
Emily Dickinson

Friendship is…

Weaving flower chains and memories

*I*t is sharing celebrations of the momentous turning points in each other's journey through life—the changing of seasons, the holidays, the anniversaries of birth, the weddings, the passage of lives.

Friends are there for us in these times of high expectations and emotions, in these moments of opening and closing, happiness and sorrow.

The marking of years—the commemorations and consecrations that glorify and sanctify being—bind with the precious and enduring ribbons of treasured memories shared.

Old friends cannot be created out of hand. Nothing can match the treasure of common memories, of trials endured together, or quarrels and reconciliations and generous emotions…We forget that there is no hope of joy except in human relations.

Antoine de Saint-Exupéry

So they went through their memories, smiling with pleasure: not the sad memories of old age, but poetic, youthful ones—those impressions of one's most distant past in which dreams and realities blend—and they laughed with quiet enjoyment.

Leo Tolstoy
War and Peace

Friendship is...

A countryside ramble

True friends share in joyous observation of the myriad of wondrous living things. Through observation comes familiarity, sympathy, affinity, and then respect. From these firm roots a beautiful friendship can flower that extends beyond our human companions to all of God's creation.

She could sit upon the low rough wall and look on and hear stories of the day. She loved this time. There were not only vegetables in this garden. Dickon had bought penny packages of flower seeds now and then and sown bright, sweet-scented things among gooseberry bushes and even cabbages and he grew borders of mignonette and pinks and pansies and things, whose seeds he could save year after year or whose roots would bloom each spring and spread in time into fine clumps. The low wall was one of the prettiest things in Yorkshire because he had tucked moorland foxglove and ferns and rock-cress and hedgerow flowers into every crevice until only here and there glimpses of the stones were to be seen.

"All a chap's got to do to make 'em thrive, Mother," he would say, "is to be friends with 'em for sure. They're just like th' 'creatures.' If they're thirsty give 'em a drink, and if they're hungry give 'em a bit o' food. They want to live same as we do..."

Frances Hodgson Burnett
The Secret Garden

"To be a good friend..." How simple it sounds—just five short words. Yet how much they represent! Think how much it could mean, a flowing out of new forces of friendship from person to person, and eventually from land to land.

Robert Hardy Andrews

The glory of Friendship is not the outstretched hand, nor the kindly smile, nor the joy of companion-ship; it is the spiritual inspiration that comes to one when he discovers that someone else believes in him and is willing to trust him with his friendship. My friends have come unsought. The great God gave them to me.

Ralph Waldo Emerson